Daniel Clement Colesworthy

A Group of Children

And Other Poems

Daniel Clement Colesworthy

A Group of Children
And Other Poems

ISBN/EAN: 9783744710688

Printed in Europe, USA, Canada, Australia, Japan

Cover: Foto ©Thomas Meinert / pixelio.de

More available books at **www.hansebooks.com**

A

GROUP OF CHILDREN

AND

OTHER POEMS.

BY

D. C. COLESWORTHY.

> THE HEART, BY SORROW PAINED AND BOWED,
> TAKES HOPE, WHENE'ER IS HEARD,
> AMID THE WORLDLY CLAMOR LOUD,
> THE POTENT LITTLE WORD.
> GEO. A. BAILEY.

BOSTON:
ANTIQUE BOOK STORE,
NO. 66 CORNHILL.
1865.

Entered, according to Act of Congress, in the year 1865, by
D. C. COLESWORTHY,
In the Clerk's Office of the District Court of the District of Massachusetts.

PRESS OF GEO. C. RAND & AVERY.

To

The Memory of

MY FATHER AND MY MOTHER

The following Pages

ARE AFFECTIONATELY INSCRIBED.

CONTENTS.

A Group of Children	9
A Little Word	22
Drops	23
Give a Trifle	26
Faults of Others	27
Looking Upward	28
Daily Trials	29
Give Every Day	31
A Present Help	33
Trifles	35
Daily Blessings	36
Patient and Strong	38
To Thee I Turn	39
Something Every Day	41
Truth	42
Little by Little	43
There is a God	46
Never say Fail	49
Read the Bible	52
Preach the Truth	55
Hidden Grief	56
Winter	57
I would Die	58
A Life among the Hills	59
It is not Wisdom	61
Don't kill the Birds	62

CONTENTS.

Epitaph	63
Triumph of Virtue	64
Charity	67
Don't be Impatient	68
Death by Intoxication	71
Sympathy	73
Be not Discouraged	74
Let us do Good	75
A Wanderer	76
Words that are Kind	77
A Lesson	79
Do not Falter	80
Suspicion	81
A Tear	82
Hymn of Gratitude	83
One Deed of Kindness	86
The Hand Divine	88
A Bitter Word	89
A Thought	90
To my Mother	91
The Acceptable Year of the Lord	96
Beauty Everywhere	96
The Rain-drop	98
My Cot	100
A Word	102
Nature Full of God	104
Heaven	107
Storm and Sunshine	109
But Once I Strayed	110
The Truth	111
Look Above	113
Epitaph	114
The Lover of Nature	115
Virtue	116
Judge not Harshly	117
Waiting and Watching	118
Not for Ourselves	120
A Smile	123
Generous and Sincere	124

CONTENTS.

Why are you Dull?	125
Triumph of the Right	127
Humble Heart	129
The Active Mind	130
Thy Brother has Fallen	133
Be mine a Cot	136
Erring Brother	137
The Mean Man	138
Ye are Going	141
Appearances	142
How to win an Erring Brother	143
Benevolence	144
Say No	145
The New Year	148
Granting Licenses	154
I love the Man	156
Death of an Only Child	159
What is it to Live?	161
This World	162
Try, Keep Trying	164
Humble Deeds	166
What is Life?	167
The Heart's Bitterness	169
The Infant Dead	170
Go not Back	171
The Good Man	174
The Great	175
Never yield to Sorrow	176
Stand Up, Brother	177
Pleasure Everywhere	179
Press On	181
Vice	182
One Fault	183
A Lesson from Nature	184
Make Others Happy	186
Rest in Peace	187
Ballots	188
Conference with the Heart	190
Rural Life	193

CONTENTS.

Stand as the Andes	195
The Desire of all Nations	197
Benevolence	199
Appearances Deceitful	200
Onward	201
We will be Heard	203
Path of Error	206
The Beautiful	207
Go Forward	208
Be Quiet	210
A Noble Example	213
Never Repine	214
One Moment	215
Mind It Not	217
Forgive thy Brother	219
Kindness	220
Our Banner	221
Keep Striving	223
I'll Never Despair	225
Smiles and Kind Words	227
Winter is Coming	229
The Blues	232
Social Prayer	234
List not to the Evil	235

A GROUP OF CHILDREN.

A GROUP of happy children see,
   With golden locks and sunny eyes;
From base intrigue—from passion free—
   Within each little bosom lies
Joy bubbling up with sweet content;
   To them each moment glides away,
Bearing afresh the lineament
   Of bliss that breathes of no decay.

How sweetly musical the gush
   Of cheerful voices on the air;
The welkin rings again; but hush!
   'Tis calm as men had met for prayer.
They shout this moment, and the next
   They're awe-struck by the sounds afar;

Now, with their little thoughts perplexed,
  Now, tongue and limbs are all ajar.

Time hastens on, and soon will each
  Gay tenant of the field and glen
The sober days of autumn reach;
  Too soon they'll grow to active men.
Their destiny I may not tell—
  Their deeds of honor and renown—
How many tears their lids may swell—
  If virtue smile, or vice shall frown.

The various paths they all may try
  To gain a living, or secure
The honors that may never die,
  I cannot see. Of this I'm sure,
If guided by an honest heart,
  A soul from vicious passions free,
Each will in life act well his part,
  And gain a blessed eternity.

A GROUP OF CHILDREN.

Perhaps amid the group I see
    One who may touch a MILTON's lyre;
A BYRON, joined to misery,
    Whose pen was dipped in gall and fire;
A LUTHER, solemn and sedate;
    A HOWARD, noble, generous, kind;
VOLTAIRE, who dared God's truth to hate,
    And trifle with the deathless mind.

That bright-eyed boy, with roguish looks,
    The midnight lamp may yet consume,
And gather knowledge from his books,
    The world of science to illume;
While he, who with a pleasant smile
    Enjoys the trifling joke so well,
May have a vicious heart of guile,
    The catalogue of crime to swell.

Yon tiny child with golden locks
    May influence yet the world at large;

Perhaps a Calvin or a Knox
  Is now beneath a parent's charge;
Or, wild and wayward, he may roam,
  An outcast on the land or sea,
Forgetting all the joys of home;—
  A wretch, despised by all to be.

He, gazing on the flashing sky,
  Or listening to the thunder-peal,
As if he felt that God were nigh,
  May have the genius of a Steele.
In him who lifts the tender flower,
  The beauteous leaves and pollen scanning,
Who loves the greensward and the bower,
  May burn the eloquence of Channing.

Beneath that noble brow, may rest
  The gentle nature of a Potts;

Or, slumbering in the generous breast,
    The deep devotion of a WATTS;
And here, a FRANKLIN's mighty mind;
    A COOPER, IRVING, or a SCOTT;
Or there, to bless the human kind,
    A DAVY, WHITNEY, or a WATT.

One, mild and gentle as he speaks,
    Preventing mischief when he can,
The welfare of the whole who seeks,
    May be a TRASK or WATERMAN:
Another, vexing all he meets,
    And sharing in the griefs of none,
Who oaths and vulgar words repeats,
    Like JEFF, may have a heart of stone.

In manners coarse and unrefined,
    Eager to catch low words of wit,
That urchin, with a groveling mind,
    Will learn to smoke and chew and spit:

The leader of a lawless throng,
    Malignant passions may control:
Oh! who can·fathom half the wrong
    That slumbers in his youthful soul?

That child, with silver voice, may be
    Like WILLIS, when he sung of yore;
A WHITTIER, modest, mild, and free;
    A BURNS, a HOWITT, or a MOORE:
In this, the flame of him who sung
    The pleasant "Voices of the Night;"
Perhaps a POLLOK, or a YOUNG;
    A SPRAGUE, a PIERPONT, or a LIGHT.

And in this little, headstrong elf,
    MONTGOMERY'S sacred thoughts may dwell;
A LADD, forgetful of himself —
    Perhaps the spirit of a TELL.

In him who shrinks from others' gaze,
   Whose angry feelings nought can stir,
The fire of passion soon may blaze, —
   More than a match for Lucifer.

Perhaps a BRAINERD's spirit may
   Rest calmly in that ragged boy;
A MARTYN, who, to give away
   The bread of life, and sin destroy
Upon a heathen shore, may yield
   The bliss of home, its pure delight;
A MUNSON, falling on the field,
   Just as the foe had met his sight.

A PAYSON, eloquent for truth;
   A JENKINS, kind, persuasive, good,
May rise from this ambitious youth,
   To stand, ere long, where erst they stood.

A RAIKES, to teach the pliant mind;
  A SCOTT, or DODDRIDGE, to expound;
A MORRISON, to lead the blind,
  Where error falls, and truth is found.

That lively boy, so full of hope,
  May be distinguished in the race;
Perhaps a GOLDSMITH, or a POPE,
  AGASSIZ, WEBSTER, or LA PLACE;
His forehead, with its full expanse,
  The living fire of talent shows;
He yet may prove a DEAN, a VANCE,
  A DRAKE, a CUTTER, or a BOZE.

Yon stately youth, with thoughtful eye
  And noble heart; frank, courteous, free;
May lay his kite and marbles by,
  A HALE, or FESSENDEN to be;
While this, impulsive, studious, grave,
  At times forgetful of his play,

May be a PREBLE, wisely brave,
   An EVERETT, SUMNER, or a FAY.

That active lad, who early fears
   Before the shrine of Vice to bow,
And marks the more than orphan tears,
   May have the earnest zeal of Dow;
In him who wanders through the fields,
   Or o'er the hills in studious mood,
While every leaf new wisdom yields,
   May live the genius of a WOOD.

And he who plays along the shore,
   While every shell his thought beguiles,
May o'er its beauties love to pore,
   Till he becomes a GOOLD, or MIGHELS:
While he who watches every star,
   When shadows gather dim and dark,
And gazes at it, bright and far,
   May have the patience of a CLARKE.

Now I behold amid the group,
    With earnest voice and flashing eye,
One whose strong spirits never droop,
    Who loves the thundering of the sky.
The whirlwind, as it sweeps the sea,
    Fixes his gaze and makes him feel
The presence of a Deity; —
    He has the spirit of a NEAL.

That laughing, witty child of fun,
    His genial brain who early racks,
Rejoicing at some mischief done,
    May be a HOOD, a HOLMES, or SAXE.
Strong for the right and fearing none,
    Yon urchin, calm, determined, strong,
May be a valiant GARRISON —
    A PHILLIPS, battling with the wrong.

Mark him with serious, solemn look,
    The Bible is his chief delight;

Each day he reads the holy book;
    He'll be an EDWARDS or a DWIGHT.
And he, to patriot pride averse,
    Full of duplicity and fibs,
May be a DAVIS, FLOYD, or PIERCE,
    A KIDD, a THORNTON, or a GIBBS.

That active wight, brimful of talk,
    Who passes all his hours so gayly,
Now swapping knives, now selling chalk,
    May be a DOWNING or a BAILEY:
While he who lingers round the hearth,
    And careful reads the choicest books,
Who will not join the pleasant mirth,
    May rise a BRYANT, or a BROOKS.

There's one who loves the ocean's roar
    And listens to the pattering rain;
He marks the waves that tumble o'er,
    And fall like giants on the main;

He's happy in the sun or shade,
    That roguish, wayward little elf;
Oh, who would think that he was made
    For NASON, BECKETT, or ourself?

The brightest of that happy throng
    No future genius may display;
Perhaps they'll school their hearts to
        wrong,
    And turn from justice, truth away;
Their crimes may stain their native land,
    To find dishonored graves at last;
Or they may join a pirate band,
    And perish, hanging to the mast.

Oh, may they all to virtue give
    Their talents and their influence now,
That in the future they may live
    With TRUTH enstamped upon the brow.

In blessing others, being blessed,
   Sweetly will pass their fleeting days,
Till in a land where spirits rest
   They tune their hearts to endless praise.

'Tis thus I muse where'er I see
   A noisy and a happy throng,
While still my spirit leaps to be
   A sharer in the sport and song.
I would I were like them again,
   So full of frolic, life and joy;
As free from sorrow, care and pain,
   As when I was a careless boy.

A LITTLE WORD.

A little word in kindness spoken,
   A motion or a tear,
Has often healed the heart that's broken,
   And made a friend sincere.

A word — a look — has crushed to earth
   Full many a budding flower,
Which, had a smile but owned its birth,
   Would bless life's darkest hour.

Then deem it not an idle thing,
   A pleasant word to speak;
The face you wear, the thoughts you bring,
   A heart may heal or break.

DROPS.

Drops of clouds are scattered freely
　　Far along the lighted sky;
Drops of sunshine, through the forest,
　　Golden strings of beauty lie.

Drops of snow and chill northeasters
　　Make the prospect dark and drear;
Drops of May-suns, and the landscapes
　　Rich and beautiful appear.

Drops of rain fall thick and faster
　　On the sunniest day in June;
Drops of rainbow beauty flashes,
　　Like an angel's noteless tune.

Drops of darkness gather nightly,
    Clothing fields and skies in gloom;
Drops of stars, in queenly splendor,
    High their golden march assume.

Drops of sorrow, daily falling,
    Mingle with life's sweetest hours;
Drops of mercy, sparkling o'er us,
    Gladden like the birth of flowers.

Drops of rancor in the bosom,
    Enter like a dagger thrust;
Drops of kindness soothe the troubles,
    Stay the war of pride and lust.

Drops of slander, rank with poison,
    Blast the sunniest joys of life;
Drops of comfort, sweet, consoling,
    Calm the angry waves of strife.

Drops of dark suspicion wither
   All the genial hopes within;
Drops of ideas, manly uttered,
   Blast the poisonous gourds of sin.

Drops of violence and hatred,
   God's creation blight and mar;
Drops of pure religion, Christ-like,
   Bring an end to rage and war.

Drops of furrows, aged pilgrim,
   Earth no longer is thy home;
Drops of faith, the world receding,
   Glory flashes on thy tomb.

Drops of death upon the features —
   Farewell to the scenes of time;
Drops of grace, the Saviour cometh,
   Soul! ascend to joys sublime.

GIVE A TRIFLE.

It is a trifle; give a mill
    To help the poor along;
'Tis not the amount, it is the will,
    That makes the virtue strong.

"I have but little," never say,
    " 'Twill not avail to give;"
A penny, if you give to-day,
    Will make the dying live.

It is the spirit, not the gold
    Upon the waters cast,
That will return a hundred fold,
    To cheer and bless at last.

Then give a trifle cheerfully
   From out thy little store;
With interest it will come to thee
   When thou wilt need it more.

FAULTS OF OTHERS.

What are another's faults to me?
   I've not a vulture's bill,
To pick at every flaw I see,
   And make it wider still.

It is enough for me to know
   I've follies of my own;
And on my heart the care bestow,
   And let my friends alone.

LOOKING UPWARD.

When I daily look up,
   And never look down,
I find that my cup
   Is filled to the crown;
Whatever is wanted
   Into my breast flows;
'Tis when the heart's lifted,
   God kindly bestows.

When I grovel in dust,
   And murmur and fret,
How few and how meagre
   The blessings I get!
'Tis only when upward
   I prayerfully turn,
That favors are granted,
   And wisdom I learn.

DAILY TRIALS.

How many sorrows daily crowd
    The fond and happy breast!
Some thoughtless friend may whisper loud
    What should not be expressed.

A harsh reply, perhaps, is made,—
    A passionate rebuke,—
When we a pleasant thing have said,
    Or others' words mistook.

For deeds of warmest charity
    Reproach may be severe;
And the sweet, pleasant smile may be
    Turned to a bitter tear.

The heart that loved us, for a bribe
    On us in scorn may turn,
Or vileness so our acts describe,
    As none the truth discern.

Such are our trials day by day —
    But he is really blest,
Whatever sorrows crowd his way,
    Or cares or pains molest —

Who watches o'er his heart with care,
    At morning, noon and night,
And lifts to Heaven the fervent prayer
    To be directed right.

GIVE EVERY DAY.

Let us give something every day
   For one another's weal;
A word, to make the gloomy gay,
   Or the crushed spirit heal;
A look, that to the heart will speak,
   Of him that's poor and old;
A tear for her, o'er whose wan cheek
   Full many a stream has rolled.

The objects of our love and care,
   In every path we see,
And when they ask a simple prayer,
   Oh, shall we selfish be,
And turn away with haughty trust,
   As if the God above
Were partial to our pampered dust,
   And only us did love?

Let us give something every day,
   To comfort and to cheer;
'Tis not for gold alone they pray,
   Whose cries fall on the ear;
They ask for kindness in our speech,
   A tenderness of heart,
That to the inmost soul will reach,
   And warmth and life impart.

Each one can give — the poor, the weak,
   And be an angel guest;
How small a thing, to smile, to speak,
   And make the wretched blest!
These favors let us all bestow,
   And scatter joys abroad,
And make the vales of sorrow glow
   With the sweet smiles of God!

A PRESENT HELP.

Call upon me in the day of trouble: I will deliver thee, and thou shalt glorify me. Psalms 1:15.

What course I take by Thee is planned,
   Who Lord of glory reigns;
Whate'er I do, thy guardian hand
   Directs, upholds, sustains.

The morning sun is not more sure
   Than thy protecting care
Of those who're in thy arms secure,
   Embraced by faith and prayer.

I will not fear when troubles rise,
   I know for all my grief
Thy love the needed grace supplies,
   And sweetly sends relief.

Should riches fail, should kindred die,
    Or those I love prove false,
I'll see the hand stretched from the sky,
    And hear the voice that calls.

That hand how dear! that voice how sweet!
    To thee, dear Lord, I'll cling,
And when life's waves most angry beat,
    Of love and glory sing.

TRIFLES.

A RAINDROP is a little thing,
   But on the thirsty ground
It helps to make the flowers of spring,
   And beauty spread around.

A ray of light may seem to be
   Lost in the blaze of day;
But its sweet mission God can see
   Who sends it on its way.

A little thought — dropped in the urn
   Of honest truth — may be
The means whereby a world shall learn
   Christ Jesus died for me.

DAILY BLESSINGS.

Day by day they fall upon me,
   Fall upon me from the skies,
Blessings, blessings, without number,
   When I rest and when I rise.

Come they in the rosy morning,
   With the gush of golden light,
When my first thank-offering rises,
   For the guarded hours of night.

In the heat of noon-day splendor,
   Blessings, blessings, still descend;
And my heart leaps joyful upward
   To my ever-present Friend.

In the stillness of the twilight,
    When is closed the busy day,
Fall they on my heart and household,
    As I lowly bend to pray.

Thus have blessings ever fallen
    From the hand above the skies,
Teaching me each moment higher
    Should the Christian strive to rise.

PATIENT AND STRONG.

When thicken the shadows,
    And darkness is spread
Where the soft golden sunshine
    So richly was shed,
Oh, look to the future,
    In a sweet, grateful song,
For the sky is all mercy —
    Be patient and strong.

The cares that distract you
    Lay resolute by,
And lift with devotion
    The heart and the eye;
And for the rich blessing
    You will not wait long,
If you are fervent and faithful,
    And patient and strong.

TO THEE I TURN.

To Thee I turn,
When sorrow droops the wing,
And winter has no spring,
And every stream is dry
That ran in gladness by —
    To Thee I turn.

To Thee I turn,
When friends I love forsake,
And bends the heart to break,
And on each face I see
The smile of treachery —
    To Thee I turn.

To Thee I turn,
In every hour of pain,
When help from man is vain,

And find a sweet relief,
While joy gives place to grief —
   To Thee I turn.

   To Thee I turn,
My Father — turn to thee ;
And love and kindness see :
When glory fills the skies —
When every pleasure dies —
   To Thee I turn.

SOMETHING EVERY DAY.

There's something every day to make
  The cheerful spirits sad —
A word to cause the heart to ache
  When it is sweetly glad.

We rise, rejoicing in the light,
  But, ere an hour is gone,
The day looks cheerless as the night
  When dismal gloom comes on.

A friend, perhaps, has treacherous proved,
  A harsh word has been said,
Or those we tenderly have loved
  Are resting with the dead.

Thus every day the heart is pained,
    By word, or look, or deed;
The real bliss that we have gained
    Proves but a broken reed.

TRUTH.

Truth will prevail, though men abhor
    The glory of its light,
And wage exterminating war,
    And put all foes to flight.

Though trodden under foot of men,
    Truth from the dust will spring,
And from the press, the lip, the pen,
    In tones of thunder ring.

LITTLE BY LITTLE.

Little fears and little sorrows
    Meet us in our daily rounds;
Little strips of golden sunshine,
    Happy birds and sweetest sounds.

Little cares and little troubles
    Mingle in our daily cup;
Little blessings, little comforts,
    In our path are springing up.

Little words, unkindly spoken,
    Sharply lacerate the heart;
Little acts of self-denial
    In each trial strength impart.

Little slanders, faintly whispered,
    Eat as doth a canker rust;
Little deeds of mercy scattered
    Bring enjoyment from the dust.

Little pains and bitter moments
    Hang with clouds the golden sky;
Little rays of mercy falling
    Drain each cup of sorrow dry.

Little fears from foes relentless
    Agitate the peaceful breast;
Little acts of Christian kindness
    Sweetly calm to quiet rest.

Little doubts of perfect safety
    Of a rest beyond the tomb,
How they fill the soul with anguish,
    And the joys of life consume!

Little glimpses of the glory
   By the death of Christ revealed,
How they dissipate the terror! —
   Make the heart rejoice to yield!

Little hours of trial ended,
   Little darkness, doubts and fears,
In a moment heaven opens,
   And the soul with Christ appears.

THERE IS A GOD.

There is a God! His voice is heard
  In every whispering breeze,
In every leaf that's gently stirred
  Upon the forest trees.
The whirlwind in its wrath and might,
  O'er-sweeping land and sea,
With desolation in its flight,
  Tells of a Deity.

The blossoms that betray the spring,
  The little birds at play,
The golden birds a-twittering
  Throughout the livelong day,
And skies that soft and mild appear,
  Whence gentle dews descend,

Tell of a God in lines as clear
   As with a sunbeam penned.

The leaves unfolding to the sun,
   In Summer's glorious reign,
Streams flashing diamonds as they run,
   Slow winding through the plain,
Or tumbling from a craggy height,
   Through groves of Araby,
So pure and musical and bright,
   Tell of a Deity.

The golden gifts — brown Autumn's pride,
   That crown the harvest-field,
The treasures that on every side
   The rain and sunshine yield,
The bearded sheaves, the bended bough,
   All eloquent exclaim,
There is a God! behold him now!
   Be thankful at his name!

The hoar-frost, and the feathery snow
    That falls so silently,
The ice that stopped the river's flow,
    Which lately dashed so free,
Careering storms and howling winds,
    The cold and piercing air,
To hearts devout, uplifted minds,
    A God! a God! declare.

There is a God! inscribed I read,
    Where'er I turn my eyes:
No less within the mustard-seed
    Than on the vaulted skies.
I cannot look below, above,
    I cannot gaze abroad,
But wisdom shines and wondrous love:
    There is, there is a God!

NEVER SAY FAIL.

Keep pushing — 'tis wiser
    Than sitting aside,
And dreaming and sighing,
    And waiting the tide:
In Life's earnest battle,
    They only prevail
Who daily march onward,
    And never say fail.

With an eye ever open,
    And a tongue that's not dumb,
And a heart that will never
    To sorrow succumb,
You'll battle and conquer,
    Though thousands assail:

How strong and how mighty,
   Who never say fail!

The spirits of angels
   Are active, I know,
As higher and higher
   In glory they go:
Methinks on bright pinions
   From heaven they sail,
To cheer and encourage
   Who never say fail.

Ahead then keep pushing,
   And elbow your way,
Unheeding the envious,
   And asses that bray:
All obstacles vanish,
   All enemies quail,
In the might of their wisdom
   Who never say fail.

In life's rosy morning,
   In manhood's firm pride,
Let this be the motto
   Your footsteps to guide:
In storm and in sunshine,
   Whatever assail,
You'll onward and conquer,
   And never say fail.

READ THE BIBLE.

Take the Bible—read the Bible —
  'Tis a precious, precious book:
Every day you scorn its message,
  Careless on its pages look,
You deprive your souls of pleasure —
  Joys which they alone can tell,
Who have found it golden treasure
  From the God of Israel.

Read the Bible—love the Bible—
  Bind it firmly to the heart;
It will cheer you in your darkness,
  And a generous light impart:
When the night of sorrow lengthens,
  Friends forsake and peace has flown,

It will chase the gloomy shadows
   With a brightness all its own.

Take the Bible — love the Bible —
   All its precepts treasure up;
And amid life's sharpest trials
   It will prove the star of hope:
In your pilgrimage 'twill cheer you —
   Shade by day and sun by night;
Joy in sorrow, health in sickness,
   Peace and pleasure, pure delight.

Read the Bible — love the Bible —
   'Tis a gift from God to man;
Every thought is inspiration,
   Breathing of redemption's plan;
And the soul, in darkness groping,
   Pointing to a region blest,
Where the wicked cease from troubling
   And the weary are at rest.

Read the Bible — love the Bible —
 Weary pilgrims, guileless youth;
Listen to its sweet instructions,
 Words of wisdom, power, and truth:
Read the Bible — love the Bible —
 Sick, in health, at home, abroad;
Every time you read its pages
 You are nearer brought to God.

PREACH THE TRUTH.

Fear ye not the face of clay,
   Preach the truth;
It will spring another day,
   If you're faithful,
And the holy Word obey.

What if scorning men oppose?
   Preach the truth,
To your friends and to your foes;
   If you're faithful,
These will yield as well as those.

With the message from the skies,
   Preach the truth,
To the foolish and the wise:
   If you're faithful,
Vice will sink, and virtue rise.

If men hear or men forbear,
   Preach the truth ;
Truth is never lost in air :
   If you're faithful,
You a crown of life shall wear.

HIDDEN GRIEF.

How oft a pleasant smile conceals
   The anguish of the breast,
Which to the joyous throng reveals
   A heart supremely blest
Ah! could we gaze within and see
   The anguish preying there,
" God, thanks for what we are," would be
   The burden of our prayer.

WINTER.

How cold it is, and dreary!
    The snow is on the ground;
The chilly north wind bloweth
    With melancholy sound.
The bright and dashing river,
    The pleasant, leaping rill,
Are touched by Winter's finger,
    And now are smooth and still.

The flowers that in the summer
    Were beautiful and bright,
And forest-trees, have perished,
    With all that gave delight.
Where'er we look around us,
    We see but stern decay:
On plain, or in the valley,
    The glory's passed away.

I WOULD DIE.

I would die when the day
  Lingers bright in the west;
When the bird hies away
  To his soft, downy nest;
When the hum of the bee
  Is not heard on the hill,
And the woodland and lea
  And the hamlet are still.

When the sad, weary heart
  Can no longer abide,
Oh, how sweet to depart
  At the still eventide!
When the sun's parting rays
  Flash glory and bliss,
And the heart is all praise:
  Be my death like to this.

A LIFE AMONG THE HILLS.

Far from the bustling, noisy crowd,
    How peaceful is the life of those
Whose names are never spoke aloud
    By subtle friends — malignant foes!
Who, unmolested in their toil,
    The pleasant seasons pass away;
Finding beneath the fruitful soil,
    Wealth to support them day by day.

I would a farmer's life were mine! —
    Oh for a home beside the hills,
Among the trees, where flocks recline,
    And the pure dew of heaven distils;
Where grateful breezes fan the cheek,
    And living blossoms scent the air;
Where vale and hill and streamlet speak,
    And the Creator's love declare.

For a secluded life I sigh:
    My soul detests the noise and strife,
The heavy air and dusty sky,
    The endless cares of city life.
To mingle with the bustling throng,
    I feel my spirit was not made;
For, when I hear the wild-wood song,
    Grandeur and love my soul pervade.

I feel at home when I can stray
    In sunny glens and dreamy woods,
And see the rippling streams that play
    Amid the lonely solitudes.
I love to linger all alone,
    And list the music of the breeze:
Sometimes a sweet and mournful tone
    It plays among the whispering trees.

A life among the hills, I ask —
    With heart, O God! devout to thee —

That I may in thy sunshine bask,
   With skies so pure and winds so free;
Where, night and morning, I can feel
   A peace within — a love to all —
With not a care my joys to steal,
   Till Thou shalt for my spirit call.

IT IS NOT WISDOM.

It is not wisdom to subdue
   A foe beneath our feet;
To cause the heart, where virtue grew,
   To practise base deceit;
To plant within the happy breast
   A thought to give it pain;
Or enter circles, pure and blest,
   An impious end to gain.

DON'T KILL THE BIRDS.

Don't kill the birds — the little birds
    That sing about your door,
Soon as the joyous spring has come,
    And chilling storms are o'er.
The little birds, how sweet they sing!
    Oh! let them joyous live;
And never seek to take the life
    That you can never give.

Don't kill the birds — the pretty birds
    That play among the trees:
'Twould make the earth a cheerless place,
    Should we dispense with these.
The little birds — how fond they play!
    Do not disturb their sport;
But let them warble forth their songs
    Till winter cuts them short.

Don't kill the birds — the happy birds
   That bless the field and grove :
So innocent to look upon,
   They claim our warmest love.
The happy birds, the tuneful birds,
   How pleasant 'tis to see !
No spot can be a cheerless place
   Where'er their presence be.

EPITAPH.

An angel, wandering from the skies,
   Beheld a jewel rare ;
And, in the tyrant Death's disguise,
   Conveyed the jewel there,
And placed it on the Saviour's breast,
To be the Prince of Glory's guest.

TRIUMPH OF VIRTUE.

No trump of fame, no clarion peal,
    Attends thy glorious reign;
No rifled fields, no hoof of steel,
    No writhing hearts of pain,
Written in blood on heaven's high arch,
Tell of thy proud, majestic march.

Thy banner is not dipped in blood
    Of children, matron, sire;
No dark, portentous horrors brood,
    With villages on fire:
Yet mighty is thy conquest now —
Before thy tread ten thousand bow.

They bow, but not the suppliant knee
   In superstitious awe;
They bow, but not in agony,
   That tyrants usurp law:
They bow to Truth, to Virtue, Right;
And rise in majesty and might.

The chains that fettered limb and mind,
   That bowed them to the dust,
And to a life of woe consigned,
   Have been asunder burst:
See what a glorious band arise,
With grateful hearts and streaming eyes!

Strong in the Right, no more the bowl
   Shall tempt from Virtue's path;
Indignant at its base control,
   Its smiles that lure to wrath,
They dash it to the ground, and swear
That truth alone shall triumph there.

Still onward roll the glorious car,
  Till not one foe remains;
Until exterminating war,
  Throughout proud Belial's plains,
Shall put each enemy to flight,
Or win him in the ranks to fight.

Onward, still onward, till the globe
  To its deep centre feels;
Till Virtue, in a golden robe,
  On fiery chariot-wheels,
Shall round the earth a glory fling,
And every heart of victory sing.

CHARITY.

When to the bosom warmly pressed,
　We take some wanderer home,
Who sought in vain a place of rest,
　Too feeble now to roam,
We but obey the voice that speaks
　From Him who rules the skies:
" He who his neighbor's welfare seeks
　Shall to my kingdom rise."

Oh, blest are they who never turn
　A brother from the door;
In every face a friend discern,
　Though feeble, sick, and poor;
And with their hands wide spread receive,
　And nurse with gentle care:
Such souls a crown of glory weave,
　In paradise to wear.

DON'T BE IMPATIENT.

Don't be impatient —
  Wait, wait, wait :
Than plunge into sorrow,
  You would better be late.
    By striving
    And driving,
The mark is not hit:
  'Tis wiser to grope,
  And feel for a rope,
Than fall in the pit.

Don't be impatient —
  Stop and think :
Better have cool moments
  On Despondency's brink,
    Than leaping
    And keeping

In water that's hot.
  'Tis wisdom to go
  On surely and slow,
Content with your lot.

Don't be impatient —
  Wait and win:
The last foe approaches,
  And the last monster sin.
    Pursuing
    And doing,
With a firm, steady eye,
  And a heart that's true,
  You'll dare and do,
And bring glory nigh.

Don't be impatient —
  Wait; be still:
Loud voice and great bluster
  Are nothing but dumb zeal;

They're louder
And prouder
Than wisdom and strength;
They rise, but, alas!
Bring nothing to pass,
And perish at length.

Don't be impatient —
Wait, wait, wait:
Than plunge into sorrow,
You would better be late.
By racing
And chasing,
You soon lose your ground:
Be patient and still;
In good time you will
With Wisdom be found.

DEATH BY INTOXICATION.

Ho! ye who for money
    The spirit imbrute,
Go look at your labor;
    'Tis terrible fruit!
You dealt him the poison,
    And bade him depart,
While the fire was burning
    The blood of his heart.

Gaze! gaze on the victim
    You poisoned for gain;
And think of his death-throes:
    Then murder again.
Be active in slaying:
    The devils in hell,
Approving, will give you
    Three cheers and a yell!

The lone wife a-weeping,
    The children in tears —
What is it but music
    To the rumseller's ears?
He feasts on their sorrows,
    Grows fat on their sighs,
And is lifted to glory
    When Misery writhes.

Gaze on the fixed eye-balls,
    So glassy and dim!
Then forth to your revels,
    And fill to the brim
The bright, fatal chalice;
    And laugh, if you please,
As you turn to the gutter,
    A brother to freeze.

Remember, men-killers,
    The day of hot doom;

When devils incarnate
   Will make for you room:
Your dark deeds of horror
   Will feed your despair,
'Mid your groans of keen anguish
   For a breath of cool air.

SYMPATHY.

There never was a human heart,
   However weak and low,
That would not generous love impart,
   And sympathy bestow,
If we ourselves should manifest
Those holy feelings in the breast.

BE NOT DISCOURAGED.

If to improve the mind, or gain
   The meed of honest praise,
Your strongest efforts seem in vain,
   Still high your standard raise:
A little knowledge gained to-day
Will greatly help you on your way.

They who on their own powers rely
   See every barrier fall:
The dauntless heart, the sleepless eye,
   Will triumph over all,
And gather round a deathless name
The victor-wreath of virtuous fame.

LET US DO GOOD.

Let us do good. How sweet the thought,
    We have the wretched blest,
Thrown smiles upon a clouded brow,
    And sunshine in the breast!

To know we've dried a single tear,
    And made one moment bright,
Or struck a feeble spark to cheer
    The darkest hour of night —

Will give to us more joy at last
    Than Cæsar's triumphs gave:
The memory of such deeds will live
    In worlds beyond the grave.

Then, in the little sphere we move,
    Let kindness touch the heart;
While every word shall lead to love,
    And happiness impart.

A WANDERER.

Wouldst thou with deep repentance
    bring
    A wanderer to the fold of God?
Use not reproach, a bitter sting,
    Nor lift to view an iron rod.

With tender words, and looks that speak
    The warm outgushings of the heart,
Go, and the adamant will break,
    And tears of true repentance start.

WORDS THAT ARE KIND.

There's pleasure in the sunshine
   That sleeps on the hill;
In the fall of the water;
   In the leap of the rill;
In the leaves that are stirring
   By the breath of the wind:
But nowhere such pleasure
   As in words that are kind.

The bright clouds that cover
   The cerulean skies,
And the autumn's sweet sunset —
   How dear to the eyes!
But brighter and dearer
   The affectionate mind,
That scatters, like sunshine,
   The words that are kind.

I love the calm waters,
    The sky and the earth;
The morning that bringeth
    Creation to birth;
Sweet bloom and rare beauty
    I everywhere find:
But these are as phantoms
    To words that are kind.

Oh! lift the dark mantle
    That shadows the heart;
And the sunshine of pleasure
    To the wretched impart:
When sorrow is pressing,
    Be ready to bind
With the love of pure virtue,
    And words that are kind.

A LESSON.

I'll teach thee a lesson :
   Be active and wise;
The deeper the valley,
   The brighter the skies;
The harder the labor,
   More weary the breast,
The sweeter the slumber
   When the pillow is pressed.

When the fierce storm approaches,
   Unbend to the blast;
Unyielding, look upward,
   Till the whirlwind has passed :
The firm and unshaken,
   Who never despair,
The seal of true greatness
   Forever shall wear.

DO NOT FALTER.

Men with sinews strong and mighty,
  Make an effort: you shall win;
  For the principle's within.
    Do not falter:
Truth will reach God's holy altar.

Dare Oppression! break her fetters;
  Fight with holy weapons; fight
  Till the dawning of the Right.
    Do not falter:
Truth will reach God's holy altar.

Lose no time in idle dreaming;
  Turn not from the cannon's blaze;
  Scorn the sword oppressors raise.
    Do not falter:
Truth will reach God's holy altar.

Up! the glorious day approaches:
　See! the victory is won;
　　God shall reign with every sun!
　　　None shall falter:
Truth has reached God's holy altar.

SUSPICION.

Hearts pure as vestal angels are,
　If dark Suspicion frown,
Will those repulsive features wear,
　Of every vice the crown.

Scorn — scorn to harbor in the breast
　This passion of the pit;
And never on a friend or guest
　In judgment dare to sit.

A TEAR.

A SINGLE tear in pity shed
   O'er sorrow and distress,
Throws sunshine round the aching head,
   To cheer, revive and bless.

One tear! who has it not to spare?
   It is a little thing,
Yet lifts the soul above despair
   On a bright seraph's wing.

Deem it not vain — a silent tear;
   But let it kindly fall:
'Twill be a gem to deck your bier
   When Death's stern voice shall call.

HYMN OF GRATITUDE.

God of the hills and verdant plains,
    I bless thy ruling hand:
The drifting snows and gentle rains
    Are sent by thy command.

The opening spring is decked by thee
    With each delightful flower;
And every leaf and bud I see
    Bears impress of thy power.

The ripening summer's burning sun;
    The winter's piercing cold;
The changing seasons as they run—
    Thy wisdom, Lord, unfold.

The joy that centres in my cot,
   No less thy wisdom owns:
With rural happiness my lot,
   I cannot envy thrones.

Love dwells within my peaceful breast
   At every morning's dawn;
And when the sun sinks in the west,
   My cares are all withdrawn.

Although secluded from the mart
   Where crowd the thoughtless gay;
Where, in the scenes that vex the heart,
   Men waste their lives away —

Beside the hill, the purling brook,
   Glad Nature's fond retreat,
With gratitude to Thee I look,
   And songs of joy repeat.

For lot so blest, my voice I raise,
    Almighty God, to thee!
Thou needest not an angel's praise;
    Much less such praise from me.

But I will bless thy bounteous hand
    For all the gifts bestowed:
Before my heart could understand,
    Ten thousand thanks I owed.

ONE DEED OF KINDNESS.

One deed of kindness every day
  Be earnest to perform:
One mite give to the poor away;
  One shelter from the storm.

One word of comfort speak to him
  Whose brow is dark with care;
One smile for her whose eyes are dim
  By sickness or despair.

One look of kind compassion give;
  One motion or a sigh;
One breath to bid the dying live;
  One prayer to God on high.

What joy one moment may impart,
   If it is spent aright!
One moment saves the broken heart,
   And puts despair to flight.

All can bestow most precious gifts —
   The weak, the low, the poor:
The feeling heart from sorrow lifts
   To heaven's wide-open door.

THE HAND DIVINE.

The impress of a Hand Divine
   On every thing I see:
The humblest flower, the tenderest vine,
   Speak of a Deity.

There's not a plant that decks the spring,
   A blossom, or a rose,
A blade of grass, an insect's wing,
   But heavenly wisdom shows.

'Twas He who gave the lily birth,
   And made the worlds on high;
In beauty spread the teeming earth —
   The God forever nigh.

'Tis everywhere I see and trace
   The finger of his love;
Whose dwelling is unbounded space,
   Around, below, above.

A BITTER WORD.

How few who speak a bitter word
   Can tell the pang it gives!
What angry feelings it hath stirred!
   What malice it revives!

Oh! let the words of kindness move
   And dwell upon your lips;
For passion, far estranged from love,
   Will brightest joys eclipse.

A THOUGHT.

If but a single thought I drop
   Into a drowsy ear,
It may revive the spark of hope,
   And the desponding cheer.

A word may save where volumes fail,
   If spoken from the heart;
And with the dying soul prevail,
   And life and strength impart.

Ye all can speak a gentle word,
   To bless the weak and low;
And o'er life's dark and thorny road
   Sweet flowers and sunshine throw.

TO MY MOTHER.

When tottering on the verge of death
   Oppressed by pain and care,
I'll place my gentle arms beneath,
   And every burden bear:
Blest guardian of my infancy,
My mother! thou art dear to me.

Thy strength is gone; and dimly burns
   Life's flickering, transient flame;
And grief and care and pain by turns
   Have paralyzed thy frame:
But, mother, on thy withered cheek
I read what language cannot speak.

And as I gaze upon thy brow,
    So wrinkled and so pale,
Where all its bloom has faded now,
    It tells a sorry tale
Of hopes expired, of joys that flew
Soon as they burst upon thy view.

For all thy care, dear mother, I
    Will bless thy life's decline,
Bring every drop of comfort nigh,
    Make all thy sorrows mine,
Till God shall break the slender thread
That keeps thee from the sainted dead.

When helpless in my infant years
    I hung upon thy breast,
Thy heart was full of gloomy fears,
    And sorrow was thy guest:
Thy child might find an early tomb,
Or stain with vice life's opening bloom.

TO MY MOTHER.

In every dark, uncertain way
   Which heedlessly I trod,
I heard thee, dearest mother, pray
   For blessings from thy God;
And, when with Folly's maze beset,
I could not all thy prayers forget.

Since thou art old, I'll guard thee well,
   And thou shalt have no care;
With years my gratitude shall swell,
   And brighter features wear,
Till Heaven life's silken cord shall sever,
And hush my voice, or thine, forever.

Till then, my fervent love to thee
   Shall strengthen day by day;
And every object I will flee
   That draws my love away;
And in these arms thou shalt be blest,
As once I was upon thy breast.

THE ACCEPTABLE YEAR OF THE LORD.
Luke iv. 19.

Joy to the world! He comes! he comes!
    The Saviour comes to bless!
Behold! the hills and mountain-tops
    Put on a glorious dress.

He comes to spread diviner light,
    And chase the thickening gloom;
To build the wastes of sin and death;
    Make deserts bud and bloom.

Lift up your hearts, ye feeble saints;
    And, with rejoicing, pray:
The promised hour is on the wing;
    He may appear to-day.

With pleading looks and ardent faith,
   And expectation strong,
Prepare to see the Saviour reign —
   The Saviour promised long.

And when he comes, as soon he must,
   Joy will your bosoms thrill;
Red war shall cease, sin be destroyed,
   And peace the world shall fill.

BEAUTY EVERYWHERE.

I see beauty everywhere —
In the earth and in the air:
At my feet, and o'er my head,
Wondrous is the beauty spread!

In the humble vine that creeps
O'er the sand — on craggy steeps —
There is something to delight,
Thrill the heart, and bless the sight.

Underneath some gray, old rock,
Hidden truth I oft unlock;
Filling me with sweet surprise —
Quickening all my energies.

In the drop that trickles down
On the dingy fence and brown,
Till it feeds the thirsty sod,
Beauteous is the smile of God.

There is beauty for us all,
On the stump or mouldy wall,
Under stones and tangled roots,
If we have not hearts like brutes.

God is good, and everywhere
Pleasure boundeth: sea and air
Runneth over with delight
To the heart and to the sight.

Earth with wondrous beauty teems,
Gushing from a thousand streams:
I will cast life's cares away,
Take my fill of joy to-day.

THE RAIN-DROP.

A LITTLE rain-drop in the sky,
    Sad and dejected, said,
"Of what use in the world am I?
    I wish that I was dead!"

It fell upon a mountain-side,
    And rolled into the sea:
A little fish the drop espied,
    And it was lost to me.

Years passed; and from the ocean's bed
    A diver careless drew
A tiny shell, which, opening, spread
    A sparkling gem to view.

'Tis worn upon a kingly crown;
  Of all, the brightest gem:
The drop that once came murmuring down
  Graces a diadem.

Weak if thou art, and sad to-day,
  Oh! never dare repine:
There is, within, a gem that may
  Yet grace a head divine.

MY COT.

My sweet little cot
   Is pleasant to me;
Where want cometh not,
   Nor sorrow I see.
'Tis hidden by trees,
   Fresh, fragrant and green;
Through which the soft breeze
   Flows musical in.

A stream runneth by,
   O'er pebbles so bright,
That they look to the eye
   Like sparkles of light.
I wonder, at times,
   If heaven can be,

With its gold and its chimes,
   More beauteous to me!

Away, pomp and show!
   No joys can ye give
Like the blessings that flow
   In the cot where I live.
And, thankful to Heaven,
   I daily look up,
In prayer that he's given
   Such joys to my cup.

A WORD.

A LITTLE word sometimes has power,
  · If it is used aright,
To make the skies that darkly lower
  Burn with a golden light.

The heart o'erburdened with distress,
  In its own dismal cell,
A word will rouse to joyousness,
  And gloom and fear dispel.

It lifts the poor from dust, and brings
  Sweet sunshine to his home;
And spreads Hope's bright, exulting wings,
  Where peace might never come.

A pleasant word, if nothing else,
  Ye all have power to give:
Make glad the hearts where sorrow
    dwells,
  And bid the dying live.

Drop pleasant words where'er ye go,
  In cot or crowded mart;
And light and peace and love will glow
  In many a wretched heart.

NATURE FULL OF GOD.

The glory of the mighty God,
   Where'er I gaze, my eyes behold;
When Evening spreads her veil abroad,
   Or morning clouds are tinged with gold.

The ocean, as it heaves and swells
   Around the isles that dot the sea,
In tones as loud as thunder, tells
   His awful power and majesty.

The stars that gem the glorious skies,
   The solemn sentinels of light,
Speak of that God which bade them rise
   To beautify the heavens by night.

The flower that smiles within the vale,
  Where careless feet may never tread,
Repeats the same unvarnished tale,
  And lowly bows its modest head.

The tiny songsters of the air,
  Which joyous float on golden wing,
The same almighty Power declare,
  And chant his praises when they sing.

The fields in verdant grandeur drest,
  In all their splendor and their bloom,
In silent language praise him best,
  And send to heaven their rich perfume.

But where is man? Has he no soul
  To speak his Maker's glories forth,
When land and sea, and orbs that roll,
  Tell of the Power that gave them birth?

Sin steels his heart, and blinds his eyes,
    And makes him careless of his God,
When all that move beneath the skies
    Conspire to sound his praise abroad.

Awake, O man! thy dormant powers,
    And let thy soul His glory sing:
Should Nature's voices rival ours
    And shame the praises that we bring?

HEAVEN.

And his rest shall be glorious. — Isa. 11: 10.

There is a glorious land afar,
Beyond the brightest burning star,
  Where peace interminably reigns;
Where soft and balmy breezes blow,
And golden rivers gently flow,
  And gladness smiles o'er all the plains.

No groveling thought, no treacherous smile,
No word unkind, no act of guile,
  Will e'er disturb the sacred rest:
On every peaceful brow will shine
A living beauty all divine,
  And love pervade the sinless breast.

The ills of life, that hover o'er
Our sunniest path, are felt no more;
   The cares of earth, a dismal train,
That follow every step we take,
Will there the happy soul forsake,
   And not molest her peace again.

At evening, when I sink to rest,
I dream of heaven, the land so blest,
   And list to hear the rapturous song.
O glorious land! I would I were
In yon pure clime a worshipper,
   Amid the bright and sinless throng!

STORM AND SUNSHINE.

How greatly wise, who never move
    When stern Misfortune lowers!
Who see the same kind hand of Love
    In sunshine and in showers!

When shadows veil the burning sky,
    Behind the clouds they know
Bright fields of golden grandeur lie,
    And seas of splendor flow.

They only bend, but never break,
    When angry storms arise;
Prepared the hand of Grief to take,
    And wait for brighter skies.

BUT ONCE I STRAYED.

One single fault forgive, I pray —
    The moments flew apace;
For, ever, where the heart is gay,
    Joy blinds the dial's face.

Fair forms were in their splendor dressed,
    And eyes were flashing bright;
And Beauty, radiant and caressed,
    Beamed as the morning light.

Forgive! it was but once I strayed:
    An angel would the same,
If in his golden walks betrayed
    By Love's enticing flame.

THE TRUTH.

The truth, the truth! oh, ever strive,
    The holy truth to gain!
Nor think the weakest efforts made
    Are ever made in vain.
Search daily in the earth and heaven,
    In Nature's works around;
Where'er a note or voice is heard,
    Or mortal footstep found.

The truth, the truth! it comes from God:
    Search deep, and find it out;
And never dare, if once convinced,
    To shut the eyes, and doubt —
Determined, if in Error's path,
    That path no more to trace,
Despite the taunts of rebel men,
    The mantle of disgrace.

The holy truth! shame, shame to those
  Who blindly lead the blind,
And shut the glorious world of light
  From the immortal mind!
Shame to the wretch, who, when he knows
  Himself he can't sustain,
With colors false, and wily words,
  Will strive his end to gain!

Thou who art Truth, teach me the truth;
  In wisdom guide, I pray;
That nearer to thyself I come
  With every rising day.
Direct, control, in every course;
  At morn, at noon, at even:
And clearer light will mark my path,
  Because it leads to heaven.

LOOK ABOVE.

When friends forsake, and health decays,
    And clouds of sorrow gather fast,
How sweet to lift the heart in praise
    To Him who loves us to the last!

When grief o'erwhelms the heart, and fear,
    Like hateful spectre, dark and grim,
To shroud our pleasure hovers near,
    How sweet to look in faith to Him!

In every lone, uncertain way,
    Amid the cares that checker life,
How sweet to look above, and pray
    For strength to bear us through the strife!

In life or death, where'er we be,
   With friends at home, or foes abroad,
With humble heart and bended knee,
   Communion will be sweet with God.

EPITAPH.

A BEAUTEOUS rose, half open, lay
   Upon its parent stem:
An angel-spirit passed that way,
   To deck his diadem;
And when he saw the lovely flower,
   " Too fair for earth!" he cries;
Then plucked it for his golden crown,
   To wear in Paradise.

THE LOVER OF NATURE.

The heart that worships tree or flower,
    Because the work of Deity,
Will find delight in every hour,
    And in all things his Maker see.

What others deem a barren spot,
    To him is clothed with matchless grace:
Where'er he steps, on hill or plot,
    A thousand beauties he can trace.

The tiny leaf, the humble weed,
    Unnoticed by the careless look,
Are pages he can daily read
    From Nature's nonpareilian book.

Full of instruction, wondrous, rare,
    Is every inch of ground he sees;
Which, studied with true Christian care,
    Brings something new to love and please.

VIRTUE.

Meek Virtue, banished from the seat
    That Wealth and Honor share,
Like flowers we crush beneath our feet,
    Sends a rich fragrance there.

They wrong who shrink from looks alone,
    Or from appearance judge:
Virtue may have the brightest throne
    In him we make our drudge.

JUDGE NOT HASTILY.

By one rash act, oh, judge him not,
   Nor cast him from your love away!
Upon his heart there's but a spot:
   All else is pure as vestal day.

Mark well his course; with steady aim
   It is the truth that he pursues:
Let not one fault turn him to shame,
   Or with the world his virtue lose.

A pitying look, a gracious word,
   May save him from the depths of woe:
Then haste with love to him who erred;
   With all a brother's kindness go.

WAITING AND WATCHING.

Be waiting and watching
  The signs of the times,
And daily keep thundering
  At the prevalent crimes:
The evils will lessen
  With every stout blow;
The brighter the weapon,
  The weaker the foe.

With words of true courage,
  March on to the field;
Determined that never
  An inch you will yield,
Till totter and crumble
  The pillars of Wrong:

'Tis Justice that maketh
   Weak instruments strong.

The Right! it must prosper,
   Whatever oppose ;
However malignant
   Or stout be its foes :
Like the steps of the morning,
   Majestic and free,
It will onward and triumph
   How gloriously !

NOT FOR OURSELVES.

"Not for ourselves," I read
   Upon the gentle showers;
Upon the fields of waving grain,
   And on the blushing flowers.
'Tis written on the glorious sun,
   "To bless the world I shine," —
On moon and stars, on every orb
   Made by a hand divine.

The happy birds that soar
   On light and golden wing —
Whene'er they grace our sunny walks,
   Not for themselves they sing.
The sparkling rivulets that leap,
   And rivers swift and strong,

Speak, in a language all can read,
  "To others we belong."

The tall, majestic oaks,
  With sturdy, iron frame,
Stretch out their arms beneath the skies,
  No glorious meed to claim.
On beasts that roam the forest wide,
  And on the finny tribe,
"Not for ourselves alone we live,"
  Doth Nature's hand inscribe.

Shall frail, dependent man,
  Casting his eye abroad,
In chains of selfishness exclaim,
  "I am creation's lord?"
And when a weaker brother calls,
  With a contemptuous glance,
"Am I my brother's keeper?" ask,
  In pride and arrogance?

If Wealth smiles at his door,
   If Plenty crowns his board,
And the delights of life are his,
   They're lent him by the Lord.
The binding duty is to give;
   His gifts with others share;
To bid the sinking captive live;
   To heal those in despair.

'Tis his to raise to life
   The feeble and the faint;
To visit prisoners in their cells,
   And list to their complaint.
In doing thus, he but obeys
   The laws of Nature's God;
And builds in heaven a throne of praise
   When sleeping 'neath the sod.

A SMILE.

A smile!—who will refuse a smile,
    The sorrowing breast to cheer,
And turn to love the heart of guile,
    And check the falling tear?

It speaks of kindness and of love,
    A generous sympathy;
And lifts, on golden wings above,
    The child of penury.

A pleasant smile for every face —
    Oh, 'tis a blessed thing!
It will the lines of care erase,
    And spots of beauty bring.

'Twill calm the passions, and subdue
 The ingrate's fiercest rage;
With buds and blossoms sweetly strew
 The path of youth and age.

GENEROUS AND SINCERE.

How pure the blessings they impart,
 Who, generous and sincere,
To lead to truth the wayward heart,
 Drop bleeding Mercy's tear!

The impulse of a love divine
 Glows in the generous breast;
And all the heavenly graces shine
 Where Virtue is a guest.

WHY ARE YOU DULL?

Why should you be dull and sad?
Nothing can be half so bad,
    We'll engage.
All is cheerful, if you look
Rightly into Nature's book,
    On each page.

Sighing, weeping, trembling — who,
When you make such loud ado,
    Will come near?
Peace and joy you drive away,
All that tend to make life gay,
    And you cheer.

It is folly, don't you know,
Thus to sink in pools of woe,
    And to weep?
Now's the time to live and and act;
Not the rust of grief contract,
    While you sleep.

From the shadows and the mire,
Up! and let the living fire
    Of ambition
Glory on your actions cast;
And, for all the guilty past,
    Show contrition.

TRIUMPH OF THE RIGHT.

Up! men of New England!
   There's no time to droop,
When the enemy cometh,
   With war-horn and troop,
To bind and enslave us,
   With shouting and blast:
Up! quick to the rescue,
   And fight to the last!

No quarter to Error!
   The skies would weep blood,
Should the efforts of freemen
   Be crushed in the bud.
Then rally your forces,
   Determined to win,

And face to lay prostrate
   The abetters of Sin.

Unsheathe from its scabbard
   The sharp, trusty sword;
And give it to freemen
   In the name of the Lord.
Command them, press forward,
   And skilfully scourge,
Till they sing, in full chorus,
   War's funeral dirge.

We know it, we feel it;
   Redemption is near:
Lo! the ranks are dissolving —
   See Justice appear,
With banners all streaming,
   And stars in her train!
Hark, hark, to the music!
   We've triumphed! Amen!

Oppression has fallen!
   Send prayers to the skies!
High let the loud anthem
   In thunder arise!
Till the earth shall re-echo,
   In strains that are meet,
To speak of a triumph
   So glorious, — complete!

HUMBLE HEART.

SHOULDST Thou bestow the power to raise
   But one petition to the skies,
I would not ask for length of days,
For wealth or honor — earthly praise;
But this my fervent prayer should be —
   An humble heart to sacrifice,
In faith and love, O God! to thee.

THE ACTIVE MIND.

What if I'm thrown upon my back?
   Must I lie still and die?
Or, cringing, ask the help of those
   Who heedless pass me by?
No! I will struggle, faint or sick,
   Upon my feet to rise:
He is a fool who hugs the sod,
   And, without effort, dies.

The active mind was never made
   In sluggish fear to rest,
When dark misfortune brings us down,
   And sorrow wrings the breast:
Up! nerved with strength, go forth again
   To battle in the strife:

THE ACTIVE MIND.

They only live who dare and do
   In every phase of life.

Who are discouraged, never win
   Bright Honor's golden prize;
Or reap the blessings spread before
   The diligent and wise.
The fair, bright sky, the broad, green earth
   Have no delights for them;
While all who pass look down with pride,
   Or scornfully condemn.

So I will persevere, if I
   A single limb can move;
Climb up, press on, should foes or friends
   Discourage or approve.
I know beyond the rolling clouds
   There is a sky serene;
And all its glories I shall view
   With not a veil between.

Eternal thanks to God, who gave
    A heart that will not cower,
In foul Oppression's darkest night,
    Beneath the foot of Power;
A heart, that when beset around
    With base, malignant foes,
Is brighter and more active found,
    The stronger they oppose.

Ay, stout and iron heart, go on!
    And never shalt thou fail:
With zeal and energy and truth
    Thou surely must prevail.
Ere long thy foes shall be subdued,
    Or in thy path be slain:
Here then I take a fresher start,
    Never to yield again.

THY BROTHER HAS FALLEN.

Thy brother has fallen!
   Oh, go to him now,
With love in thy bosom,
   And smiles on thy brow.
Speak words of true kindness,
   And bid him arise
From error to virtue,
   And press to the skies.

Thy brother has fallen!
   Assist him to stand;
Throw round him thy mantle;
   Extend him thy hand:
Be gentle, be tender,
   Persuasive and kind;

And to his heart's centre
   A way thou wilt find.

Though sunk and degraded
   By error and vice,
Till early affections
   Are cold as the ice,
Compassion and kindness,
   Once felt in the heart,
Wilt melt to contrition
   By the warmth they impart.

Thy brother has fallen!
   Oh! hasten to give
The help that is needed,
   And bid him to live.
Wait not for the morrow:
   To-day is the time,
Before he is hardened
   In error and crime.

Ask not for the reason
   That brought him so low;
That he is disgraced is
   Sufficient to know.
When virtue has triumphed,
   Joy beams in his eye,
With tears he will bless thee,
   With hands to the sky.

To save a lost brother,
   What honor so great?
Yet thousands neglected
   Are left to their fate,
When a word — a look even —
   Would virtue restore,
And keep the lost brother
   From wandering more.

BE MINE A COT.

Be mine a cot beside the hill,
    Where summer winds are free;
And, musical, a gentle rill
    Flows onward to the sea:
Where birds of varied hue shall sing
    Their earliest, sweetest lay;
And flowers, warmed by the breath of spring,
    Their richest dress display.

Such cot be mine: I ask but this,
    With Ellen by my side,
To make this earth a scene of bliss,
    To bliss of heaven allied.

Each season in its round would be
  With thousand blessings fraught;
And not a morning dawn on me
  That care or sorrow brought.

ERRING BROTHER.

He cannot know the human heart,
  Who, when a weaker brother errs,
Instead of acting Mercy's part,
  Each base, malignant passion stirs.

Harsh words and epithets but prove
  That he himself is in the wrong;
That first he needs a brother's love
  To touch his heart and point his tongue.

THE MEAN MAN.

The mean, the despicable wretch!
    Whom all on earth despise:
The rich man turns from him in scorn;
    The good, the learned, the wise,
Avoid his presence; and the poor
    Thank God they're not like him.
He has no friends, though he has power
    In perfumed baths to swim.

The mean man! Day and night he strives
    To break his neighbor down;
Alike unheeding Wisdom's voice,
    And Anger's scathing frown.
No sympathy can move his heart,
    No sorrow bring a tear;

And when he wrings the generous heart,
   Satanic smiles appear.

The mean man! Mark his half-shut eye,
   His staid and shriveled look:
Pure Love could find no virtue there,
   And cheek and eye forsook.
She left the lineaments of ill,
   A genius to destroy,
And never touched that brow again
   With sunshine or with joy.

The earth, all rife with bud and bloom,
   So beautifully bright,
And happy birds, with golden plume,
   Tinged by the morning light,
Look dull to him: he cannot see
   That Beauty smiles around,
And breathes in every leaf and flower,
   And trills in every sound.

THE MEAN MAN.

The mean man! See! he gropes along,
    A vile and hated thing!
His presence turns delight to fear,
    Makes gloom and sorrow spring
In circles of the young and gay,
    And throws a shadow dark
O'er every blessed scene in life
    By comfortless remark.

The mean man! God of heaven! I pray
    His life may ne'er be mine;
That kindness, virtue, love and truth,
    In all my conduct shine;
For others' woes that I may feel,
    And soothe the laboring breast:
Who make their neighbors' grief their own,
    Themselves are doubly blest.

YE ARE GOING.

Ye are going, ye are going
    To the grave —
One and all, the prince and beggar,
    High and low,
    Weak and brave,
    Fast ye go
To the grave, the grave, the grave.

Time is flying, time is flying!
    Oh, prepare
For the grave that now is yawning!
    Hale in years,
    Young and fair,
    Fools and seers,
For the grave prepare, prepare!

Do not linger, do not linger
    By the way;
For apace the tyrant cometh:
    List! his tread,
  Night and day,
    With the dead,
To hurry you away, away.

APPEARANCES.

'Tis not the loftiest looks betray
  A heart that's free from guile;
For, where the foulest passions prey,
  The practised lip may smile.

The noble, generous, and the wise,
  With no attractive grace,
May be commissioned from the skies,
  A blessing to the race.

HOW TO WIN AN ERRING BROTHER.

Speak not in anger, if from sin
You would an erring brother win:
If you a sinner would reclaim,
A wild, unbridled spirit tame,
Use gentle means, a pleasant word,
And kind emotions will be stirred.

A brother, when he goes astray,
Is more determined on the way
When he beholds an angry face,
And never may his steps retrace;
But, when he sees a tearful eye,
Turns back with deep humility.

Speak, then, in kindness: love alone
Must to an erring friend be shown;
The warm, kind heart, the feeling soul,
The angry waves of sin control,
And lead to duty and to truth
The hoary sinner, wayward youth.

BENEVOLENCE.

It is a little thing to give
   A cup of water to the poor,
Or spare a morsel to relieve
   The famished stranger at the door;
And yet these trifling favors may
   Return to bless ere life shall close,
And cheer through earth's dark, devious way,
   If multiplied should be our woes.

SAY NO.

When tempted to wander
    From duty and truth
By the siren of pleasure,
    In the hey-day of youth,
Have courage to answer
    The soft-smiling foe
And, prompted by virtue,
    Decided, say No!

When the glass that is sparkling
    Is pressed to the lip,
And jovial companions
    Invite you to sip,
Beware of the serpent
    Beneath the rich glow,

And dash the bright wine-cup
   With a hearty No, no!

The gamester may track you
   With his treacherous wiles,
With words that are pleasant,
   And a face wreathed in smiles;
In sport he may ask you
   The dice-box to throw:
Be firm in your virtue;
   Indignant, say No!

The way that is infamous
   What multitudes throng,
With music and dancing,
   And soul-melting song!
'Tis Beauty bewitching
   Invites you to go:
Away from false splendor,
   Say heartily, No!

Oh! ponder your footsteps,
  Leap not in the dark,
Upon a wild ocean
  Launch not your frail bark,
Without that true wisdom
  Which God can bestow:
When beckoned by Error,
  Decided, say No!

Take, take the good Bible
  For your guide and your chart;
And bind its pure precepts
  Close, close to the heart.
If then you are tempted,
  To God you will go;
And strength will be given
  For a hearty No, no!

THE NEW YEAR.

OLD TIME has taken another step,
    And brought the New Year round:
We see it in the leafless trees,
    And on the silver ground.
The streams that sparkled in the sun,
    And joyous leaped along,
Now bear upon their glassy breast
    A buoyant, happy throng.

The flowers, bright, beautiful and gay,
    That decked the hill and dale,
Have hastened to a quick decay;
    And Autumn, chill and pale,
Has scattered Summer's beauties round;
    And desolation drear

Broods over all that blessed the eye —
   Gave rapture to the ear.

O Time! O Time! what glories fall
   Beneath thy giant tread!
A few brief months, and teeming life
   Lies withered, blasted, dead!
The birds that caroled in the grove
   Their sweet, mellifluous lay,
Like the bright leaves that sheltered them,
   Have passed like them away.

Oh! pleasant were the summer hours,
   As to the woods we hied,
When all the trees and all the flowers
   Were in their glowing pride.
Joy gushed from every vein to hear
   Sweet Nature breathing round,
And every breeze bore to the ear
   Music's voluptuous sound.

They've gone — the music and the birds,
    The flowers and waving trees:
They've passed like infants' happy dreams;
    And brighter things than these
Have perished with the rolling year.
    The friends — oh! where are they,
Who blessed the sunny walks of life?
    The noble, generous, gay?

Full many a hearth is desolate,
    And many a heart is sad:
We look for those, but look in vain,
    Who made our spirits glad:
Beneath the cypress and the sea,
    Nought shall their slumbers break,
Till the last awful trump shall sound,
    And bid the dead awake.

The year! how pregnant 'twas with joy
    To many hearts allied,

That hardly dared to dream of bliss,
    Lest evil should preside!
Courage and fear alternate took
    Possession of the breast:
Sometimes a whisper, then a look,
    Gave pleasure, or depressed.

Now union and a happy life
    Dawn on the youthful pair:
The mutual cares, the mutual joys,
    'Tis their delight to share.
Oh envied lot! and yet, and yet
    To sorrow they are doomed:
An early blight has often chilled
    The brightest flowers that bloomed.

Wise Providence! that thus conceals
    The shafts that hover near!
That rend in twain the noblest hearts,
    And sunder ties most dear!

Could we foresee the thousand ills
    That in our pathway lie,
" O God!" might be our earnest prayer,
    " Permit us now to die."

How many circles, fond and blest,
    Have been to grief a prey,
Where bright and beauteous plants have been
    Torn suddenly away!
The cheerful voice, the pleasant smile,
    The noble heart, and kind,
We look for — but we look in vain;
    The lost we ne'er shall find.

Change, change, marks the revolving year,
    Change is on all impressed :
Our friends, ourselves, how soon may we
    In death's cold slumber rest!

Though nerved with strength, in life's full
    bloom,
  We must, we must obey
The awful mandate, " Dust to dust,"
  ·And mingle clay with clay.

So be it ours to live, that when
  Our course is finished here,
We may to brighter worlds ascend,
  Where Virtue's sons appear;
And, in the presence of our God,
  Enjoy the bliss supreme,
Studying the wonders of his love —
  The holy angels' theme.

GRANTING LICENSES.

The damning story must we tell,
While loud exult the imps of hell,
   That Christian men in Christian times,
Discarding reason, virtue, law,
Have opened Hades' bloody maw,
   And bartered souls for rusty dimes?

Unheeding sighs and tears and groans,
That start to life indignant stones,
   Ye crush the hopes, and force the blood,
And scatter far the seeds of ill;
For gold, determined that ye will
   Plant death where virtue strives to bud.

Ye dare, beneath Jehovah's eye,
His love deride, his wrath defy :
  And, when he speaks in thunder out,
Attempt to baffle his design,
And intercept, where Truth would shine ;
  Then o'er God's blasted people shout.

The brown old earth in sorrow lies,
Huge tears drop from the sable skies,
  And moans the breeze along the shore :
Ye've cursed the land God made so bright,
Extinguished Reason's glorious light,
  While Nature bleeds at every pore.

As if the pace of Sin were slow,
Ye bid the world to ruin go,
  And on the blasting misery feed :
Red hell grows warmer with your praise,
And demons chuckle as they gaze
  Upon the dark and damning deed !

I LOVE THE MAN.

I LOVE the man who calmly rests,
    When wealth and friends are flown;
Who Virtue, Truth, — those heavenly
        guests, —
    Securely makes his own;
Who never looks to earth for bliss;
    Whose treasure is the skies;
To whom keen Sorrow's dark abyss
    Brings no depressive sighs.

I love the man who kindly bears
    The haughty tyrant's frown:
Alike to friend and foe he wears
    The look of calm renown.
The proud contempt, the conscious slight,
    Do not affect his soul:

He's firmer in the truth and right
  When Passion's billows roll.

I love the man who freely gives
  As Heaven has blest his store;
Who shares the gifts that he receives
  With those who need them more;
Whose melting heart of pity moves
  O'er sorrow and distress;
Of all his friends, who mostly loves
  The poor, the fatherless.

I love the man who scorns to be
  To name or sect a slave;
Whose soul is like the sunshine, free —
  Free as the ocean wave;
Who, when he sees oppression, wrong,
  Speaks out in thunder-tones;
Who feels, with Truth, that he is strong
  To grapple e'en with thrones.

I love the man who shuns to do
    An action mean or low;
Who will a noble course pursue
    To stranger, friend and foe;
Who seeks for justice, not for gain;
    Is merciful and kind;
Who will not give a needless pain
    In body or in mind.

I love the man whose only boast
    Is wisdom, virtue, right;
Who feels, if truth is ever lost,
    His honor has a blight;
Who ne'er evades by look or sign,
    In weal or woe the same:
Methinks the glories are divine
    Which cluster round his name.

DEATH OF AN ONLY CHILD.

Light footsteps at the door I hear:
   I raise the latch, and look.
My bright-eyed boy! thou art not there:
   Returning with his book,
Another child, less fair than thou,
Smiles as he passes by me now.

Falls on my ear a gentle tone,
   As through the crowd I press:
'Tis not thy voice, dear cherished one!
   Like thine, would it were less!
And then this heart, so big with grief,
Would not in tears find such relief.

A gentle hand hath pressed my cheek
  While in my study-chair :
I seemed to hear thee sweetly speak,
  "My father, I am here;"
When lo! I saw another child,
Who only mocked me as he smiled.

When dimly burns the chamber light,
  I kneel beside thy bed;
I seem to hear thy sweet "good-night,"
  But tears profusely shed,
While on that couch I look, where lay
So lately he now passed away.

And in the morning, when I rise,
  I hasten to the room;
But oh, the truth! it drowns my eyes —
  "Your idol cannot come;"
And then the agony I feel,
No soothing words of love can heal.

Whene'er I see a happy boy,
   Sadly it speaks of thee —
A mother's love, a father's joy,
   All that a child could be —
Sleeping beneath the valley's clod :
How could it be ? my God ! my God !

WHAT IS IT TO LIVE?

What is existence, but to give
   Our influence to a righteous cause ?
To bless the world, and thus receive
   The heart's affections, not applause ?

To live is but an empty name,
   Our lives a blot to truth and right,
When vicious men our deeds proclaim,
   And Justice weeps at Virtue's flight.

THIS WORLD.

'Tis beautiful! 'tis beautiful!
    This glorious world of ours;
Life-teeming slopes and waving fields,
    And bright, delicious flowers.
We cannot look, but Beauty lives,
    And in her splendor reigns;
On shrubs and trees, on seas and lakes,
    On mountains and on plains.

This world is beautiful; but oh!
    Would it not be more fair,
If Pride and Hate, and Envy dark,
    Wan Sorrow and dumb Care,
Were not companions by the way,
    At morn, at noon, at even?

Were sin unknown, would not earth be
    The vestibule of heaven?

When every thing is beautiful,
    Oh! why will man do wrong?
Nor look upon the glorious world
    With grateful heart and tongue?
When Gladness springs in every path,
    Joy floats on every breeze,
With Pride and Folly fetter-bound,
    God's smile he never sees.

Each bird and tree and blushing flower,
    Each rill that leaps along,
Seems with a music-voice to pour
    An ever-grateful song.
Awake, O man! with Nature round
    So beautiful and bright,
Lift up thy soul in gratitude,
    And share the pure delight.

TRY, KEEP TRYING.

HAVE your efforts proved in vain?
Do not sink to earth again;
  Try, keep trying:
They who yield can nothing do;
A feather's weight will break them thro';
  Try, keep trying:
On yourself alone relying,
You will conquer; try, keep trying.

Falter not! but heavenward rise!
Put forth all your energies;
  Try, keep trying:
Every step that you progress
Will make each future effort less;
  Try, keep trying:

On the truth and God relying,
You will conquer; try, keep trying.

Ponderous barriers you may meet,
But against them bravely beat;
    Try, keep trying:
Nought should drive you from the track,
Turn you from your purpose back;
    Try, keep trying:
On yourself alone relying,
You will conquer; try, keep trying.

You will conquer if you try,
Win the prize before you die;
    Try, keep trying:
Remember, nothing is so true,
As they who dare will ever do;
    Try, keep trying:
On yourself and God relying,
You will conquer; try, keep trying.

HUMBLE DEEDS.

It is not those who make a boast
    Of generous deeds which they perform,
Who for the needy do the most,
    And find them shelter in the storm.

He who has never raised his voice
    To gain the plaudits of a crowd
Has often made the hearts rejoice
    That with oppressive chains were bowed.

In humble life meek virtues spring
    To glad the heart, to bless and cheer,
That never fly on eagle's wing,
    Or on the printed page appear.

WHAT IS LIFE?

AND what is life, if we alone
    Live to promote vile, selfish ends?
If our ambition is a throne,
    Regardless of our foes or friends?
It is not worthy of the name,
    And better that we perish now,
Than kindle Honor's lurid flame,
    Or to the god of Passion bow.

'Tis only real life, when we
    Fill up our days with noble deeds;
Pluck from the breast of Poverty
    Dark Melancholy's fruitful seeds;
And, where the hand of Sorrow pressed,
    Put efforts forth to cheer and heal,

And plant within the torpid breast
   A lively faith — a holy zeal.

They who the mandate of the great
   Upon a trembling throne obey,
Who for his beck and nodding wait,
   From fiery youth till life is gray,
Are abject slaves, and never know
   The glories of a freeman's life;
The joy and peace and love that flow
   In vales secure from pain and strife.

Oh! wouldst thou live, and living bless
   The sons of woe? and pour within
The lonely heart of deep distress
   The oil of joy? to virtue win
The men of crime? turn straight away
   From gilded honors, worthless fame;
For these but crumble to decay
   Before the light of Virtue's flame.

THE HEART KNOWETH ITS OWN BITTERNESS.

Whene'er we see a happy face,
   How little do we know
Within the breast how large a space
   Is filled with grief and woe!

Perhaps a pleasant smile conceals
   A pang which none discerns;
And, while the brow a joy reveals,
   The fire of anguish burns.'

Oh! could we read the inmost heart,
   Its sorrow and its grief,
Back from the smiling face we'd start,
   And seek to give relief.

Pity instead of hate would move,
  And love inspire the breast:
A thousand times we should approve
  Where censure is expressed.

THE INFANT DEAD.

Happy infant! early blest!
Sleeping on thy Saviour's breast.
Pains are ended, tears are dry:
Oh, how blessèd thus to die!
Though we mourn, we would not bring
Shadows to thy cherub wing,
And to earth return again
Sister of an angel train.
Bowing low, we kiss the rod:
'Twas in kindness sent by God.

GO NOT BACK.

My brother, go not back;
    The pledge is taken now:
I see it in the healthful smile
    That plays upon thy brow;
I see it in the sparkling eye,
    So dull and dim before:
Then go not back again, my friend,
    To sure Destruction's door.

My brother, go not back;
    Press on in Virtue's way:
Be steadfast in thy sacred pledge,
    And Truth shall be thy stay;
Hope, bright as morning's dawn, shall spring
    Where'er thy feet may tread:

Then go not back again, my friend,
    To paths of terror spread.

My brother, go not back
    To sorrow and to vice;
To reap the bitter fruits of sin,
    Where none to glory rise;
Where, stranger to the joys of earth,
    Life will be steeped in woe:
Then go not back again, my friend;
    But upward, heavenward, go.

My brother, go not back;
    The fatal whirlpool see,
Where thousands and ten thousands rush
    To hopeless misery.
Behold them perish day by day,
    Unconscious when they sink:
Then go not back again, my friend,
    To Ruin's fearful brink.

My brother will not go:
  I read it on his cheek;
I see it in the tears that flow,
  And when I hear him speak.
He has resolved, in God's own strength —
  Who will, I know, sustain —
Never, while Reason holds her throne,
  To touch the cup again.

THE GOOD MAN.

Within his ever-peaceful breast
    No angry feelings rise:
Contentment is his constant guest,
    And every want supplies.

If blest with wealth, he daily gives
    The needy at his door;
If poor, he thankfully receives,
    Without a grasp for more.

While others murmur or complain,
    With joy he looks abroad,
And in the sunshine and the rain
    Sees the kind hand of God.

In pleasantness and peace his days
  Pass happily away;
Angels, approving, on him gaze,
  And round his dwelling stay.

THE GREAT.

Who are the great? The great are they
  With hearts from pride and envy free;
Who ne'er unholy power obey,
  Nor bow to wealth the suppliant knee;
Who covet not the applause of men,
  Are happy in an humble sphere,
And never, with the lip or pen,
  Debase the heart or pain the ear.
If called to rule, no selfish aims
  Prompt them to stand in Honor's seat;
True glories cluster round their names,
  While grateful hearts their worth repeat.

NEVER YIELD TO SORROW.

Though clouds obscure the summer sky,
    Yield not to dark despair;
The glorious sun is just as nigh
    As when the skies were fair.

As many sorrows press our way,
    When laughter fills the breast,
As when we yield to stern dismay,
    And all in gloom is drest.

We make the pangs we daily feel
    Our sorrow and our grief,
When, should we bid our fears be still,
    Joy would give quick relief.

STAND UP, BROTHER.

Stand up, brother! here's the hand
That will help thee rise and stand;
Here's the heart that warmly burns
When a prodigal returns.
    Stand up, brother!
For a friend thy spirit yearns.

Stand up, brother! stand upright!
Let the scales fall, see the light;
And no longer in the dust
Let thy mind be clogged with rust.
    Stand up, brother!
And the galling fetters burst.

Stand up, brother! fear no ill;
We will love, protect thee still:
When the night of darkness lowers:
In the tempest's strongest hours.
    Stand up, brother!
These are warm, kind hearts of ours.

Stand up, brother! yes, thou wilt,
Though so long oppressed by guilt:
On thy brow we gladly read,
"You have been my friends indeed."
    Stand up, brother!
We are just the friends you need.

PLEASURE EVERYWHERE.

There's pleasure everywhere
  To hearts that rightly feel;
And no one need complain of care,
Or on his brow a sorrow wear,
  Or painful thoughts reveal.

Nature below, above, —
  How beautiful to view!
In every path we choose to rove,
We find a thousand things to love,
  Each wonderful and new.

Then be not sad, I pray:
  The earth, the sea, the sky,

Are clothed in smiles; and, full of play,
The beasts and birds wear time away;
   Then why not you and I?

A glorious world is ours,
   In peerless beauty dressed;
With trees and shrubs and blushing flowers,
O'er which the sunlight falls in showers,
   And slumbers on its breast.

PRESS ON.

Press on, press on to virtue,
    Until the goal is won;
Nor linger with the farewell beams
    Of the departing sun.
Move limb and heart; go forth
    With majesty and might;
And never tire and never faint,
    At daybreak or at night.

Press on, press on to virtue;
    The prize you'll win at last,
If with a courage unsubdued,
    And firm truth buckled fast,
In Heaven's high name you go.
    As sure as morn succeeds
The night, so sure on Glory's page
    Will burn Faith's noble deeds.

VICE.

A MONSTER grim and awful 'tis,
   Black as the noon of night;
With horrid brow and demon phiz,
   And eyes of sulphurous light.

Beneath a fair and lovely mask
   His ugly form he hides,
While smiling he pursues his task,
   And thoughtless wretches guides.

Along the path to infamy
   He strews the sweetest flowers,
O'er which he spreads a gorgeous sky,
   A sky that never lowers.

'Tis thus the ruin he completes
    Of those who yield to sin:
His presence like a canker eats,
    When all seems peace within.

ONE FAULT.

They little know the human heart
    Who for one fault a friend forsake,
And from the law of love depart,
    Indifferent though that heart should break.

One fault — oh! hide it from the gaze
    Of those who rise when virtue sinks!
This course that noble mind displays
    Which at God's fount of mercy drinks.

A LESSON FROM NATURE.

Behold the sky! how glorious 'tis,
    In gold and silver dressed;
As if the sunny vales of bliss
    Were opening on the blessed.

Behold the earth! a glory crowns
    The lowland and the lea,
The hill-tops and the plumy downs,
    Each leaf and shrub and tree.

Behold the beast! in shady groves,
    Or resting by the stream,
Where'er the forest tenant roves,
    There's happiness for him.

Yet thou art sad. O man! awake,
    And cast thy sorrows by;
Of earth's full happiness partake,
    Nor waste thy strength and die.

Heaven made thee for a happy man,
    To be supremely blessed;
Yet thou wilt thwart his wondrous plan,
    In clouds of gloom depressed,—

In clouds of gloom, when all around
    Is cheerful, happy, bright!
Up from the shadows on the ground,
    To wisdom, life and light!

MAKE OTHERS HAPPY.

I would not on a happy face
   A shade of sorrow bring,
Nor in a gentle bosom place
   A vicious thought to sting.

I would not cause from laughing eyes
   A single tear to start,
Nor rouse forgotten memories
   To shade the sunny heart.

I deem it sin, when we can light
   The thorny path of gloom,
And make the cheek of sorrow bright,
   The tearful eye illume,

A word to breathe, a look to cast,
   That stings a human breast,
Or make a painful feeling last,
   When life should all be blest.

REST IN PEACE.

The turmoil of the world is o'er;
   In quiet rest thee now:
Thy generous heart no envy bore,
   No stain was on thy brow.

Soft Pity was thy constant guest;
   Thy bosom, Mercy's throne;
And every place thy presence blest
   With heavenly radiance shone.

BALLOTS.

The heart of oppression
   To crush or subdue,
Cast prayerful your ballots,
   O patriots true!

These dumb little missiles
   The citadel rock
Where the mother of Treason
   Had nurtured her flock.

In terror they scatter
   The plots of the base,
And scathe as with lightning
   Proud Tyranny's race.

The ballots of freemen —
   How nobly they speak!
Giving hope to the fallen,
   And strength to the weak.

They speak to the bondmen, —
   Lo! Freedom has come!
They speak to the tyrants, —
   Oppression is dumb!

To the ballot-box rally,
   Each patriot son!
With numbers and union
   The victory is won!

CONFERENCE WITH THE HEART.

Yield not, stout heart, to dark despair!
   O'er every foe thou'lt triumph yet,
And on thy front the victory bear,
   Before the sun of life is set.
Shall look or word, shall face of clay,
   Thy courage daunt, or quench thy zeal,
Or from thy duty turn away?
   Must all thy talents slumber still?

Fear not, stout heart! press on, press on,
   Undaunted, till each foe is slain,
Or powerless from the field is gone,
   With all his vile, malicious train.
What are the puny arms that wage
   War with the sacred truth and right,

Compared with those who dare engage
   To fall or conquer in the fight?

Up with thy courage! there is nought
   That can a warlike soul alarm:
The future is with glory fraught
   For quenchless zeal and sinewy arm.
Up from the dust! and break the chain
   That binds thy spirit to the earth;
And never dare to sink again,
   Forgetful of thy noble birth.

To yield to sorrow and dismay,
   And sigh and weep o'er blessings past;
To turn from truth and God away,
   And all thy sacred honors blast;
To move along in doubt and fear,
   And tremble at the shades of even, —
What is it but a tomb to rear,
   And, stealing to it, turn from Heaven?

Up, then, stout heart! and know thy
    power,
  And dissipate the mists of ill :
Should still the storms of terror lower,
  Press on, thy duty to fulfil.
Press on! dig through the barriers thrown
  Across thy path by envious hands ;
For, lo! the victory is thy own,
  Where Truth complete in armor stands.

'Tis energy with faith that springs
  In the stout heart, until it rise,
From dust and sin, on angel's wings,
  And gives it life beyond the skies.
I see them go, the shadows fly,
  Bright hope beams beauteous from
    afar,
A cloud of glory fills the sky,
  And wisdom burns in every star.

RURAL LIFE.

How pleasant is the slumbering vale,
   Where winds are blowing free,
And gifts of Nature never fail!
   Oh, such a home for me!

There songs of birds delight the ear,
   And flowers rejoice the eye,
And beauty lingers all the year
   On water, field and sky.

Such home be mine, among the hills,
   The giant forest-trees,
Where leap along the flashing rills,
   And fragrant is the breeze;

Where voice profane and boisterous song
    Will never taint the air;
And few are taught to practise wrong,
    Or breathe a selfish prayer.

To city life I bid adieu;
    Its crowded mart, farewell!
With rural scenes, forever new,
    My spirit longs to dwell.

Sweet, oh, how sweet! at morn and eve,
    To cast the eye abroad;
Pure truths from Nature's voice receive,
    And humbly worship God.

STAND AS THE ANDES.

Stand firm as the Andes,
    Determined and strong,
When the waves of corruption
    Are surging along.
Face manfully error,
    And never turn back,
Though the fagot is blazing,
    And frowning the rack.

Stand firm as the Andes,
    In turbulent times,
When Error with Virtue
    Exultingly chimes,
And prostrate is Mercy,
    And Wisdom is fled,

And the spirit of Devotion
  Is chilled as the dead.

Stand firm as the Andes,
  When Treachery, rife
With all that is evil,
  Is seeking your life;
When foes are increasing,
  And bearing you down,
And every face weareth
  Revenge or a frown.

Stand firm as the Andes,
  Nor flinch at the blast:
Though Justice may slumber,
  It waketh at last.
The foe shall lie prostrate,
  When Heaven decree,
And Right be triumphant,
  And all shall be free.

THE DESIRE OF ALL NATIONS.

And I will shake all nations, and the Desire of all nations shall come. — HAGGAI 2: 7.

HARK! hark! the glad tidings!
   The Saviour appears!
O'er error triumphant,
   His kingdom he rears.
Lo! tumble the mountains,
   And tremble the hills,
As the sweet song of gladness
   The universe fills.

The Saviour! how glorious
   His face to behold,
And feast on the blessings
   That never were told!

And list to the music
   That rolls from the skies,
As the songs of devotion
   Like incense arise!

Up, sinner redeemed!
   The Saviour embrace,
And press like a soldier
   In the van of the race;
And he will infold thee
   In the arms of his love,
And bless thee, and take thee
   With the ransomed above.

BENEVOLENCE.

Benevolence, like sunshine, sheds
    Her grateful beams o'er all,
Supplying food and downy beds
    Quick to the sufferer's call.

She visits prisoners in their cells,
    And generous gifts bestows;
Where sorrow pines, or misery dwells,
    The tear of pity flows.

Where evil lurks, with friendly voice
    She warns of danger nigh,
And a sweet influence employs
    To draw men to the sky.

Among the blessings thou dispense,
  Deny me not, O Lord!
A heart of true benevolence,
  While faith leans on thy word.

APPEARANCES DECEITFUL.

'Tis not in hearts that seem to feel
  That kindliest feelings are possessed:
Where efforts are put forth to heal,
  There is the sympathizing breast.

Loud words and actions may appear
  As if a noble work were done;
While Mercy, in an humble sphere,
  Asks and receives the praise of none.

ONWARD.

With Onward! your motto,
    You never will fail,
Should Poverty track you,
    Or Envy assail.
No obstacles hinder,
    No trials molest,
Whose aim is still upward,
    With truth in the breast.

The shadows that mist-like
    Hang under the sky,
And hide the bright prospects
    Behind them that lie,
Will fold with the darkness
    Their wings for a flight,

And glory and beauty
  Give only delight.

The sorrows you cling to
  Were never designed
To tax or to fetter
  The high-gifted mind:
'Twas made to soar upward
  With angels and God,
And not to be trammeled
  On the valley's cold sod.

Then onward! See blazing
  Away in the sky
The motto so glorious,
  " Look up, and not die!"
'Tis the language of angels,
  Of men who can feel,
When the world they would startle
  In thunder appeal.

WE WILL BE HEARD.

Our cause is just — we will be heard,
    Whoever may oppose;
Our weapon Truth, our watchword Right,
    We'll manly face our foes.
God did not with his image stamp
    The living, deathless mind,
That man control it at his will,
    And into atoms grind.

The waves that beat upon the shore,
    In thunder speak, *We're free!*
So gentle airs, careering winds,
    And every thing we see.
We will speak out, and man shall hear —
    The truth is unconfined:

Proud, haughty tyrants fall before
   The majesty of mind.

You say we're weak : grant it be so,
   If outwardly you judge ;
But look within ! what read you there ?
   Not made to be a drudge.
You may confine the limbs, and think
   That earnest thoughts will rest :
Aha ! you never can destroy
   The freedom of the breast.

Slaves, slaves, you call us, and you dare
   Upon our lips to place
Foul hands to smother burning words;
   Because God gave our race
A feeble arm ; but know, ye men
   Of but a transient might,
Our wrongs shall speak, and earth and heaven
   Respond unto the Right.

WE WILL BE HEARD.

We will be heard; we will be free;
    You cannot bind us long:
Go chain the ocean, lightning chain,
    And you may hold them strong;
But oh! the bright, immortal Mind,
    With God's own nature free,
Leaps forth majestic in her strength
    To compass land and sea.

Our cause is just; it will not sleep;
    From dust we shall arise:
The strength we seek is not of earth —
    'Tis kindred to the skies.
When slumbering Justice is aroused
    In wisdom and in might,
Then woe to all who dare oppose
    The dawning of the Right.

PATH OF ERROR.

How dark and fearful is the path
   That leadeth man astray!
No blushing flowers to love it hath;
   No beauty spreads its way.

The light that in the distance burns
   Eludes the wanderer's eye:
'Tis but a meteor he discerns,
   That flashes on the sky.

Bright, beautiful, the opening seems,
   In gorgeous splendor dressed:
'Tis like the sun's departing beams,
   When lingering in the west.

They linger but to leave behind
    More dark and threatening clouds :
Error entices but to blind,
    And then each hope enshrouds.

THE BEAUTIFUL.

The lovely and the beautiful —
    How soon they fade away!
The hearts we loved and cherished most
    First hasten to decay.

Heaven, partial to the fairest flowers,
    Transplants them to the skies,
To beautify the golden walks
    Of his own paradise.

GO FORWARD.

Go forward, press onward:
   'Tis wiser, by far,
Than fretting and sighing
   In fear where you are.
Whatever your calling,
   Your aim or pursuit,
In hand with true Wisdom,
   You'll bear precious fruit.

A Putnam and Warren —
   What made them to be
Remembered forever
   By the good and the free?
'Twas active exertion,
   Indomitable zeal,

And minds that were tempered
   With wisdom and steel.

Go forward, press onward:
   Oh, live not in vain!
There's wisdom, and honor,
   And glory to gain.
The path is before you,
   You've only to choose:
You win if you're active;
   If slothful, you lose.

Go forward, press onward:
   A moment's delay
May thicken the shadows
   That rise o'er your way.
This waiting and wasting
   The summers that fly
Will leave you a sluggard
   To linger and die.

BE QUIET.

Be quiet; don't murmur,
    Nor sink in the dust;
The good day approaches,
    When onward you must:
Your fears cast away,
Be cheerful and gay;
Look up and look on,
Soon night will be gone.

Be quiet: stop weeping,
    And keep a good heart,
Each morning and evening,
    To take a fresh start.
Within and about
Keep a sharp lookout,

That nothing betray
Or block up your way.

Be quiet, be earnest:
   A purpose so high
Should give you true courage,
   And make you defy
The storms that approach,
And foes that encroach,
To darken your skies,
Or close Reason's eyes.

Be quiet, be watchful:
   There's peril each hour
In the glow of the sunrise,
   In the smile of the flower,
In the dew of the even,
In the breezes of heaven,
On the lip, in the eye:
Watch, — danger is nigh.

Be quiet, be patient:
   The still are the sure;
While others are grasping,
   The prize they secure.
Blind haste and quick zeal
To passion appeal,
And raise a loud storm,
But nothing perform.

Be quiet; don't murmur:
   Work fairly and slow,
And daily in wisdom
   And power you'll grow;
Accomplish whatever
In heart you endeavor:
No honor comes late
To the watchful who wait.

A NOBLE EXAMPLE.

When bleeding Mercy from the skies
    Assumed a human form,
He came to bid the helpless rise,
    And hide them from the storm.

The fire of love in Jesus's breast
    Shone steady, pure, and bright:
The sick were healed, the sorrowing blest,
    The blind restored to sight.

To save from sorrow and despair
    Was Christ's sweet mission here;
And all who breathed to him a prayer
    Found him a Friend most dear.

Oh, blest example! May we strive
  To open Mercy's door,
And bid the dying sinner live,
  And all to heaven restore!

NEVER REPINE.

At the sorrows that fall,
  I never repine;
I know they are all
  From a Father divine:
I feel his kind care,
  And duty perform;
And his blessing I share,
  In sunshine and storm.

ONE MOMENT.

Now is the accepted time. — 2 Cor. vi. 12.

One moment, thoughtless sinner, spare,
   To seek the grace of Heaven;
One moment lift in earnest prayer
   For sins to be forgiven.

One moment to thy Maker give,
   Amid the waste of time;
One moment cease in sin to live,
   And taste of joys sublime.

One moment step thy foot aside
   From Error's fatal way,
And ask the Saviour's care to guide
   Through life's uncertain day.

One moment: can it be too much
   To give the Lord divine,
Whose gracious smile and gentle touch
   Will melt that heart of thine?

One moment give, — beyond all price
   A blessing will descend,
A title clear to paradise,
   And joys that never end.

One moment spare — oh, spare to-day!
   One moment give to Heaven;
One moment, sinner, stop, and pray,
   "Lord, be my sins forgiven."

MIND IT NOT.

Is the tongue of slander loose?
    Mind it not.
What avail is low abuse?
Go ahead, and do not stop
For the words the rabble drop.

With a steady heart and eye,
    Mind it not.
Strength of purpose will defy
All the shafts of bitter hate
Aimed at your devoted pate.

Point the finger, if they will:
    Mind it not.
At your purpose, and be still;
Silence writes the epitaph
Quickly of the scornful laugh.

Do they crowd you? — keep your hold:
    Mind it not.
In the right you can be bold,
On a firm foundation stand,
Though men fall on either hand.

When or howsoe'er assailed,
    Mind it not.
"He is fearful, he has quailed,"
Let it not of you be said,
Till the vital spark has fled.

FORGIVE THY BROTHER.

Forgive thy brother who has erred,
    And take him by the hand;
And, as you speak a generous word,
    Assist his feet to stand.

Joy sparkles in his eye to hear
    Thy words of gentle tone:
Forgiveness breathed upon his ear,
    And love and kindness shown,

Will make him rise to life again,
    And shun the path he trod,
When in the round of Folly's train
    He broke from Truth and God.

Forgive thy brother, — even now
   A smile is on his cheek;
The glow of heaven has tinged his brow:
   Speak, and forgive him; speak!

KINDNESS.

In every breast, however rude,
   There is a glow of love,
A latent spark of gratitude
   That words of kindness move.

If every pain and care we feel
   Could burn upon the brow,
How many hearts would move to heal
   That strive to crush us now!

OUR BANNER.

The star-spangled banner,
   So nobly unfurled,
To the breezes of heaven,
   Is the hope of the world.
Of old did our fathers
   Protect it with blood;
And, battling with tyrants,
   Unflinching they stood.

Up! up with the banner —
   We solemnly swear,
Protected by Heaven,
   No tyrant shall dare
Strike the stars that are burning
   So gloriously bright,

Or stain with dishonor
  Its halo of light.

The star-spangled banner,
  The flag of the free,
And the pride of our nation,
  Forever shall be.
No despot shall seize it,
  No tyrant molest,
While the heart of a freeman
  Beats warm in the breast.

KEEP STRIVING.

Keep stirring and striving —
   The day will soon dawn,
When night and oppression
   Will break and be gone;
When darkness and error
   Will sink to the shade,
And Vice, hoary-headed,
   Be still and afraid.

Be patient and active —
   Oh, deem it not vain
If but an inch foot-hold
   In a year you obtain:
The good time approaches,
   When Truth will go forth,

And leap like the lightning,
    From the South to the North.

Keep stirring and striving —
    Lose nought by delay,
Nor sit aside trembling
    At the drones in the way:
Good thoughts may be scattered,
    And borne on the wind,
To soften and influence
    The prejudiced mind.

Keep pushing and striving —
    Lo! tremble and fall
The pillars of Error,
    Foundation and all!
Jehovah, who blesses
    The just and the right,
Has come in his power,
    His wisdom and might!

I'LL NEVER DESPAIR.

How golden the motto,
  "I'll never despair!"
Within the heart's centre
  I'll treasure it there:
    In sorrow and pain,
    Fools only complain;
  I'll never despair.

When shadows and darkness
  Hide glories that were,
And hope flies the bosom,
  I'll never despair,
    But rise, and rejoice
    With Nature's glad voice,
  And never despair.

When trials are pressing,
  I'll joyfully bear,
And wait for the blessing,
  But never despair:
    The sun will illume,
    And chase the thick gloom,
  If I never despair.

Right onward and upward,
  With prudence and care,
I'll mock at and conquer
  The demon Despair:
    Look never behind,
    And glory I'll find,
  If I never despair.

SMILES AND KIND WORDS.

When the heart is dejected,
   And pleasure is flown,
And passed the bright moments
   So fondly our own,
And stilled is the music
   Of nature and birds,
How sweet to the bosom
   Are smiles and kind words!

The fond heart is breaking
   In burning despair,
While clothed in broad sackcloth
   Are skies that were fair:
Oh! save, ere it perish,
   The sorrowful mind,

By smiles that are pleasant,
   And words that are kind!

I've been to the palace
   Of the rich and the gay,
Where the sirens of pleasure
   Chase sorrow away;
But never, oh! never
   Such joys have I seen,
As gush from the bosom
   Where kind words have been!

WINTER IS COMING.

Winter is coming, cold and drear —
    See ye the poor around?
Oh! when the wrathful storms career,
    And snow o'erspreads the ground,
Will ye not take them by the hand,
    Or to the hovel go,
And round the dying embers stand,
    And wipe the tears that flow?

Winter is coming — hear ye not
    The mother's earnest cry?
For dark and dreary is her lot, —
    No real friend is nigh.
For wood and bread she asketh now:
    Oh! shall she ask in vain?

WINTER IS COMING.

See sorrow stamped upon her brow,
    And mark the orphan train.

Winter is coming — every drawer
    Should be unlocked to-day:
Whom do you keep that clothing for?
    Why not give it away?
Come, pull it out! a cloak, a vest:
    Whatever you can give,
Wrapped snugly round the orphan's breast,
    Will make the dying live.

The closet search — a pair of shoes
    Half worn; and here's a cap,
Which you, perhaps, may never use;
    A hat with scarce a nap,
A pair of pants, a rusty coat —
    Oh, give them to the poor:
What is not worth to you a groat
    Will warmth and health secure.

What's in your attic? Have the moths
   For months been busy there?
Ay, they have quite destroyed the cloths
   You saved with prudent care.
Come, pull them out: perhaps we may
   Find something that will make
A poor man rich if given to-day,
   And bless the hearts that ache.

Winter is coming — give, oh! give
   Whatever you can spare:
A mite will make the wretched live,
   And smooth the brow of care.
When plenty smiles around your door,
   And comfort dwells within,
If you neglect the worthy poor,
   'Twill be a grievous sin.

THE BLUES.

Oh! do not unwisely
   Sink down in the mire,
And dream that the mountains
   Frown darker and higher;
That the whirlwind is coming
   In wrath and in might;
That wild clouds are meeting
   For long, endless night.

The shade and the valley,
   Why should they be thine,
Where birds never linger,
   And suns never shine;
Where the leaf and the blossom,
   The stream and the spring,

To the eye and the bosom
   No pleasure will bring?

Up! forth to the hillside
   Where buttercups bloom,
And dandelions scatter
   Their gold and perfume;
Where blossoms are floating
   Like butterflies' wings,
And the sweetest of songsters
   Right merrily sings.

Up! forth to the hillside,
   And never again
With a shade on thy forehead
   Look down and complain.
A stroll in the sunshine
   Past vigor renews,
Brings joy to the bosom,
   And scatters the blues.

SOCIAL PRAYER.

Father, we meet, a little band,
   In Jesus's name to pray :
The blessing of thy grace command,
   And turn us not away.

We would be more like him we love,
   And less to sin inclined :
Our best affections place above,
   And peace and pardon find.

When Jesus deigns to be our guest,
   How sweet the moments fly ! —
True love beams brightly in the breast,
   And all "see eye to eye."

LIST NOT TO THE EVIL.

List not to the evil
   That Malice has spread;
And coals that are burning
   Heap not on his head:
If erring, forgive him,
   Nor take him to task
The moment he ventures
   For mercy to ask.

Who has not departed
   From Truth and from God?
Who knows not the anguish
   Of contempt and the rod?
Be gentle, be tender;
   Encourage him now,

And the penitent smile
  Will flash on his brow.

Oh! what if like mountains
  His past errors rise?
Forgive him the moment
  Tears drop from his eyes;
And never in anger,
  Ill-will, or in pride,
Recur to the vices
  'Tis virtue to hide.

THE END.

www.ingramcontent.com/pod-product-compliance
Lightning Source LLC
Chambersburg PA
CBHW031749230426
43669CB00007B/546